3 0117 90251 1217

KT-420-394

WITHDRAWN

Frankenstein

Mary Shelley

Level 3

Retold by Deborah Tempest

Series Editors: Andy Hopkins and Jocelyn Potter

Pearson Education Limited

Edinburgh Gate, Harlow,
Essex CM20 2JE, England
and Associated Companies throughout the world.

Pack ISBN: 978-1-4058-8446-4
Book ISBN: 978-1-4058-8398-6
CD-ROM ISBN: 978-1-4058-8397-9

First Penguin Readers edition published 2000
This edition published 2008

3 5 7 9 10 8 6 4

Text copyright © Penguin Books Ltd 2000
This edition copyright © Pearson Education Ltd 2008

Illustrations by Ignacio Noé

The author has asserted her moral right in accordance with the
Copyright Designs and Patents Act 1988

Set in 11/13pt A. Garamond
Printed in China
SWTC/03

Produced for the Publishers by AC Estudio Editorial S.L.

*All rights reserved; no part of this publication may be reproduced, stored in a retrieval system,
or transmitted in any form or by any means, electronic, mechanical, photocopying,
recording or otherwise, without the prior written permission of the Publishers.*

Published by Pearson Education Ltd in association with Penguin Books Ltd,
both companies being subsidiaries of Pearson Plc

Acknowledgements

We are grateful to the following for permission to reproduce photographs:

Page 74 © **Bettmann/Corbis**

Every effort has been made to trace the copyright holders and we apologise in advance for any
unintentional omissions. We would be pleased to insert the appropriate acknowledgement
in any subsequent edition of this publication.

For a complete list of the titles available in the Penguin Active Reading series please write to your local
Pearson Longman office or to: Penguin Readers Marketing Department, Pearson Education,
Edinburgh Gate, Harlow, Essex CM20 2JE, England.

Contents

	Activities 1	iv
	The First Letter	1
Chapter 1	Young Frankenstein	3
Chapter 2	Frankenstein Creates Life	8
	Activities 2	16
Chapter 3	William Is Dead	18
Chapter 4	Frankenstein Finds the Monster	23
	Activities 3	26
Chapter 5	The Monster's Story	28
Chapter 6	The Monster Wants a Wife	33
	Activities 4	40
Chapter 7	Frankenstein in England	42
Chapter 8	Another Murder	48
	Activities 5	52
Chapter 9	Frankenstein in Prison	54
Chapter 10	Back in Switzerland	57
	Activities 6	60
Chapter 11	Elizabeth	62
Chapter 12	The End of the Monster	67
	The Last Letter	70
	Talk about it	72
	Write about it	73
	Project: A New Heart	74

1.1 What's the book about?

1 *Frankenstein* is a famous story. In it, a man makes a terrible monster from parts of dead people. But which of these pictures shows Frankenstein? Tick (✓) the box.

2 Discuss these questions.

    a Have you seen a film about Frankenstein? What happens in it?

    b Do you think this book will have a happy or a sad ending? Why?

1.2 What happens first?

1 Look at the words in *italics* at the top of page 1 and at the picture on page 2. Frankenstein is telling Robert Walton the story of his life. What do you think he has lost?

2 Compare the pictures on pages 2 and 4. How is Frankenstein different? Where do you think he is in each picture? Make notes.

Notes

        Picture, page 2   Picture, page 4

The First Letter

*'You have hope,' he said to me. 'You have no reason to be unhappy.
But I have lost everything...'*

My dear sister Margaret
I am writing to you from my ship. We have travelled a long way, and we are now in the far north. It has been a difficult and dangerous journey, but we are safe. There is ice all around the ship and it is very cold. We are waiting for an improvement in the weather before we continue.

I have something interesting to tell you. A few days ago, we found a man in the sea. He was travelling across the ice, but his dogs died. He was alone. We were hundreds of miles from land, so we were very surprised.

'Where are you going?' he asked. He was from a foreign country, but he spoke in English. I told him about our journey to the North Pole*.

The man climbed onto the ship. He was half-dead with cold and tiredness. He was thin and ill and could not say very much. We took him to the kitchen so he could warm himself. The poor man was completely frozen. We gave him dry, warm clothes. Then he ate some soup and slept.

Now our strange visitor feels better. He is a very interesting man, but he is very unhappy. He wants to come to the North Pole with us. He often looks out into the water. He is looking for something – or somebody. I do not know who he is. But I can see that he has suffered terribly. His eyes are sad and sometimes he seems quite crazy.

At first, I did not want to ask him too many questions. He seemed very nervous. Then, when he was not so hungry and cold, we had some interesting conversations. I started to like the man and I wanted to be his friend. He has a quick and intelligent mind. I told him a little about myself. He knows now that I left England on my travels six years ago. And here I am, looking for the North Pole. I will not return home until I succeed.

* The North Pole: the most northern place in the world.

'You have hope,' he said to me. 'You have no reason to be unhappy. But I have lost everything and I cannot start life again.' He looked extremely sad as he said this. Then he was silent and went to bed.

Yesterday, the man promised to tell me about his life.

'My story is very strange, sad and frightening. But perhaps people will learn something from it,' he said.

I have decided to write it all down, in his own words. When I have done that, I will send it to you. I know it will be very strange, Margaret. But I think it will also be very interesting.

I will write to you again soon,

Your loving brother
Robert Walton

2

CHAPTER 1

Young Frankenstein

*I was interested in the secrets of the sky and the earth,
of the natural world.*

My name is Victor Frankenstein. I come from Geneva, in Switzerland, and my family is one of the most important in that country. When I was very young, my parents travelled a lot. I was their only child, and they took me with them. My parents were kind and they loved me very much. My earliest memories are happy ones.

When I was about five years old, we stayed for a week at Lake Como in Italy. My mother was a kind woman and visited a poor family on a farm. They had five children. Four had dark hair like the man and his wife, but the other child, a girl, had fair hair and looked quite different. The farmer's wife told my mother the child's history.

The girl's name was Elizabeth Lavenza, and she was the daughter of a rich man from Milan. Her mother died when she was born. Elizabeth's father died too, trying to free his country from a bad government. He lost everything – his house and his money. It was all taken away. His child was left with this family.

My mother wanted to have another child very much. And she wanted a daughter. When she saw Elizabeth, she loved her immediately. She wanted to bring Elizabeth up as her own child. She talked to the farmer and his wife about her idea. The farmer and his wife loved the girl, but they agreed. They were not rich. They wanted Elizabeth to have a good life. So they agreed that the child could live with us.

Everyone loved Elizabeth. She and I were brought up together, and she was like a sister to me. We were good friends and never fought. The differences between us brought us closer together. Elizabeth was calm and happy. She enjoyed reading poems and she loved the mountains around our home in Switzerland. I was interested in facts. I wanted to discover everything about the world around me. The world, to me, was full of secrets, and I wanted to find the answers to them.

My parents then had another son, Ernest. He was seven years younger than me. Later, another brother was born. His name was William. We stopped travelling and moved to Geneva. We also had a country house at Belrive, on the eastern side of the lake. Belrive was away from the city and we enjoyed a quiet life there. We spent more and more time at the country house. I became close friends with a boy called Henry Clerval. He was the son of a businessman from Geneva. He was a very clever boy and he read a lot of adventure stories.

I was extremely happy as a child. My parents were always kind to us. They did not have many rules and we always enjoyed ourselves. We could do what we liked. Life was amusing and fun.

But my mind was full of questions. I wanted to learn, not to play children's games. I read a lot of books on science. The most interesting subject to me was **chemistry**. I was interested in the secrets of the sky and the earth, of the natural world. My friend Henry was interested in history, adventures and dreams. Elizabeth loved us and had a very kind heart. Her goodness shone like a light in our calm, pleasant home. Her smile, soft voice and beautiful eyes brought happiness to our lives.

chemistry /ˈkemɪstri/ (n) an area of scientific study

One day, when I was about fifteen years old, we saw a terrible storm at our house in Belrive. It came from behind the mountains. I stayed and watched it with excitement. As I stood by the door, I suddenly saw a stream of fire pour from an old and beautiful tree. It was about 60 feet from our house. When the **lightning** disappeared, only the bottom of the tree was left. The tree was completely destroyed.

After that, I never forgot the **power** of the lightning. I was very interested in electricity, and in the power that exists in all natural things. I wanted to learn more about different kinds of science. So I started to study these subjects with even more excitement than before. At that time, perhaps, an idea began to form in my mind. But that idea brought only **misery** to my later years.

lightning /ˈlaɪtnɪŋ/ (n) bright electrical light in the sky during a storm
power /ˈpaʊə/ (n) the ability of something to destroy. When you have *power* over someone, they have to follow your orders.
misery /ˈmɪzəri/ (n) great unhappiness

When I reached the age of seventeen, my parents decided to send me to the University of Ingoldstadt. But before I left, a terrible thing happened. It was the first of many terrible things that happened in my life.

Elizabeth became very ill and her life was in danger. My mother did not want to leave Elizabeth's bedside. She looked after her day and night. After three days, Elizabeth got better but then my mother quickly became very ill too. We soon realized that she was dying. As she lay in bed, close to death, she took my hand and Elizabeth's hand.

'Children,' she said, 'I am putting all my hopes in the two of you. I want you to marry. I believe that your marriage will bring you future happiness. It will make your father happy too. Elizabeth, my love, I want you to take my place. Look after my younger children. I am sorry that I am leaving you all. It is so hard. But I must hope that I will meet you in another world.'

Without my mother, the house was empty and cold. Elizabeth was very sad, but she helped me and the rest of my family. We tried to forget about death; we had to live for the future. Elizabeth was sweet and kind to us, and I loved her very much.

The day came when I had to leave for Ingoldstadt. Henry Clerval spent the last evening with us. He could not come to university with me, because his father wanted his son to work with him. It was difficult for me to leave my best friend. We did not want to say goodbye. But in the morning they were all there – my father, Henry and Elizabeth. They watched me leave and I promised to write.

I arrived at Ingoldstadt and started studying. I was good at science and decided to give all my time to it. On my first day, my new teacher, Mr Waldman, told me to forget everything that I already knew.

'If you want to become a real scientist,' he said, 'you must learn all the sciences. But I want to teach you chemistry. That is an area of science that is growing. We are discovering new things all the time. So it is a very important subject.'

I listened carefully to Mr Waldman. He took me to his **laboratory** and showed me his **experiment**s. I was very excited by everything that I saw. Mr Waldman gave me a list of new books to read.

At the end of the day, I was tired but happy. I will always remember that day, because it decided my future.

---

laboratory /ləˈbɒrətri/ (n) a room or building where scientists do tests
experiment /ɪkˈsperɪmənt/ (n) a scientific test to discover something

CHAPTER 2

Frankenstein Creates Life

Nervously, I used my tools to create life inside the body.
Then I saw his yellow eyes open.

I became a good student. From the first day, chemistry was my favourite subject. Mr Waldman was an excellent teacher and I met the other scientists at the university. I worked on experiments in the laboratory all the time. Sometimes I stayed there all night until the stars disappeared from the sky. In the mornings, I was tired but happy. I went to my lessons, read a lot of books and understood more and more.

For two years I worked hard and did not visit Geneva. I wanted to discover where life came from. I wanted to experiment with science as much as possible.

I wanted to **create** life. But first I had to understand death. I studied the **human** body. I also studied dead bodies. I was very interested in the change from life to death. I saw how a body changes. I learned how bodies are made.

And what was the result of all my experiments? I discovered the secret of life. I learned how to create life. I was very surprised and extremely happy. At first, I did not know what to do with my new powers. I could create life, but life needs to be inside a body. So I went to hospitals and looked at more dead bodies. I took parts of human bodies back to my laboratory. After a few months, I began to create a human form.

It was difficult work. I decided to make the person very large and tall. It was easier to work on a large body. I worked in secret in my laboratory at the top of the house. The summer months passed. The weather was beautiful, but I never went outside. I was too busy. I did not want to stop my work for anything. I

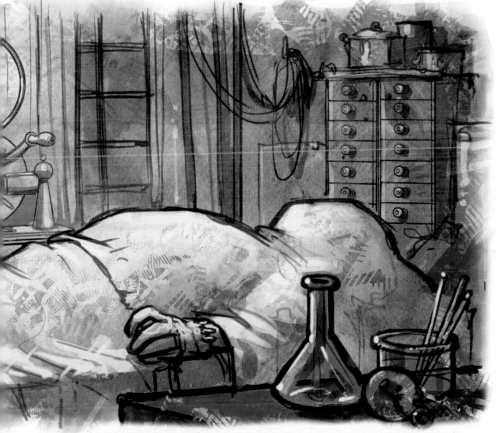

create /kri'eɪt/ (v) to make something new
human /'hju:mən/ (n/adj) a person (man, woman or child)

forgot about my friends and my family. I did not write to them. I knew that my father and Elizabeth and Henry worried about me. I received letters, but I did not answer them. I thought only about my experiment.

Autumn came. My work was nearly finished, but my health was not good. I could not eat or sleep. I did not talk to anyone. Every night I felt ill and very nervous. I was afraid. But I could not stop.

One cold night in November, I saw the first result of my hard work. The body of the man in front of me had no life in it. It was one o'clock in the morning, and rain was falling outside. Nervously, I used my tools to create life inside the body. Then I saw his yellow eyes open. He **breathe**d and moved his arms and legs.

Success! The body was moving. After years of work, here was a human life! I looked at him. How can I describe my feelings? The man was terribly ugly. He had thick black hair and white teeth, but his skin was yellow and dry. His eyes were very pale. He was a **monster**.

After nearly two years of this experiment, I looked at the ugly monster and misery and fear filled my heart. My dream disappeared. I ran out of the laboratory and went to my bedroom. I threw myself on the bed and tried to forget about the monster.

But when I fell asleep, I had wild dreams. I thought I saw Elizabeth. She was walking in Ingoldstadt. When I kissed her, her mouth became cold. It was like a kiss of death.

I woke up, shaking with fear. The yellow light of the moon was shining through the window, and the monster was standing next to my bed. He looked at me. His mouth opened and he made some sounds, but I could not listen. The monster touched my arm, but I escaped from him. I ran downstairs, out of the house, and stayed away until early morning. Then, slowly, I went inside and listened for every sound. I did not ever want to see him again. I felt fear and misery. But I was also very sad. My dream was dead, and my hopes were destroyed.

At six o'clock I went outside again, for a walk. The sky was black and it was raining heavily. I was afraid to go back to my room. So I continued walking and got wetter and wetter. I came to a hotel and waited outside for a few minutes. Then I saw Henry Clerval.

'My dear Frankenstein,' he cried, 'I am so glad to see you! I have just come from Geneva. At last, my father has given me permission to study at the university here.'

breathe /briːð/ (v) to take air into your body and let it out again
monster /ˈmɒnstə/ (n) a large, ugly, frightening person or animal in stories

For the first time in many months, I felt happy and calm. I welcomed my friend happily. I took his hand and in a few minutes I forgot all my misery. We walked towards the university together. 'I am very pleased to see you, Henry,' I said. 'Tell me about my family. How are my father and brothers? And Elizabeth?'

'Very well, and very happy. But they are worried because you do not write to them.' Henry stopped and looked at my face. 'My dear Victor,' he continued, 'you seem so thin and pale – so ill. You look tired. Have you been awake all night?'

'You have guessed right, Henry. I have been very busy with one piece of work. I have not rested enough. But I hope that this work is now finished. I am free.'

We arrived at the door of my house. I did not want to see the monster. I did not want Henry to see it. So I told Henry to wait at the bottom of the stairs. I

went up to my room and I opened the door slowly. I went inside, but it was empty.

'The monster has run away,' I thought. I could not believe my good luck. My enemy was not there.

I went downstairs to get Henry. We went to my room and had breakfast. But I could not sit at the table. I was so happy. I jumped over the chairs and laughed wildly.

'My dear Victor,' Henry cried. 'What is the matter? Do not laugh like that. You are ill! How did this happen?'

'Do not ask me,' I cried. Then I thought I saw the monster in the room. I put my hands in front of my eyes. 'Oh, save me!' I shouted, and fell on the floor.

This was the beginning of a long nervous illness. For many months, Henry was my only nurse. He did not tell my family about my illness. He did not want to worry them.

During my illness, I talked about the monster. Henry could not understand me. He believed that I was imagining strange things. But I returned to the same subject again and again. He realized that it was not a dream. There was a terrible reason for my illness.

Slowly, Henry brought me back to good health and I became calm again. One day, when I looked out of the window, I noticed new leaves on the trees. It was spring. I felt much better.

'Dear Clerval,' I said, 'how can I thank you? You have been so kind to me. You came here to go to university. But you have been a nurse all winter. I am very sorry.'

'It does not matter, Victor,' he replied. 'You do not need to thank me. I will be happy if you are well. That is enough for me. But promise me one thing. Please write a letter to your father and to Elizabeth. You have been silent for a long time, and they are very worried about you. They do not really understand how ill you have been.'

'Of course I will,' I replied. 'They are the most important people in my life. They are always in my thoughts.'

'Then maybe you are well enough to read this.' Henry gave me a letter. 'It arrived a few days ago.'

It was from Elizabeth, and it was a very kind, friendly letter. She told me about my father and my brothers. She asked me to write back. I was very happy to read her letter, and I wrote back immediately.

Two weeks later, I was able to leave my room, and I returned to the university. But I did not want to study science now. I took everything out of my laboratory. When I saw my chemistry equipment, I felt very nervous again. I hated chemistry.

Henry did not like science. He wanted to study foreign languages. I was very happy to study with him and I enjoyed my new classes. I did not want to leave Henry alone in a place he did not know very well. So we spent the summer together happily and I decided to return to Geneva at the end of the autumn. I was ready to go home.

Winter arrived, and there was a lot of snow. The roads were terrible. It was impossible to travel and I had to wait until the spring.

The month of May arrived. I waited for a letter from my father before I decided on a date for my return. While we waited, Henry and I went on a holiday. We walked in the countryside around Ingoldstadt. It was very beautiful, and we enjoyed ourselves. Henry was an excellent friend to travel with. My health was much better now. The blue sky and lovely green fields made me strong. When we arrived back at the university, we both felt calm and happy.

2.1 Were you right?

Look back at your answers to Activity 1.2, 2. Then circle the right answers.

1   Robert Walton first meets Frankenstein near *Geneva / the North Pole / London*.

2   Victor Frankenstein sees the storm at his house in *Geneva / Ingoldstadt / Belrive*, in Switzerland.

2.2 What more did you learn?

1   Put the right names in these sentences.

A   She lives with Victor's family but she is not his sister.

Her name is ....

B   There are three brothers in Victor's family. The youngest brother

is called ....

C   Victor has a good friend when he lives at Belrive and later at university.

His name is ....

D   When Victor goes to university, his very interesting science teacher is called

....

2   Look at these pages from Victor's science notes. Write in the missing words.

November 4:

TODAY, at last, my big
experiment is a success.
I have worked for ....
years, day and ....
I have studied the human
body, ... and dead.
I have discovered the
.... of life. I took
.... of dead bodies
from the hospitals to my
.... I ....
the parts together and made
a very large, tall body.

Last night the body began
to live and ....
It opened its pale ....
and moved its ....
and legs. Suddenly I saw that
this was a terrible, ugly
.... I ran out of the
laboratory.

Now I don't know what to do.
I have .... something
that really frightens me.

2.3 Language in use

At university, Victor has a lot of questions in his head. Later, when he is telling his story, he talks about them. Look at the sentence in the box. Then read Victor's questions and write similar sentences.

I wanted to discover **where life came from.**

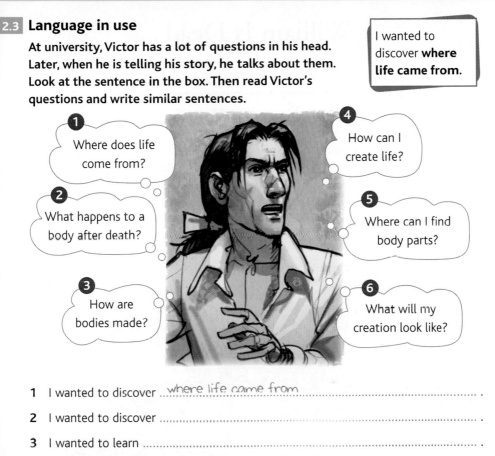

1 Where does life come from?

2 What happens to a body after death?

3 How are bodies made?

4 How can I create life?

5 Where can I find body parts?

6 What will my creation look like?

1 I wanted to discover ...where life came from.. .

2 I wanted to discover ....

3 I wanted to learn ....

4 I wanted to learn ....

5 I wanted to know ....

6 I wanted to know ....

2.4 What happens next?

Frankenstein has created a monster and it has disappeared. Slowly, he has become happier. But terrible news is coming. What do you think it is? Read the first sentence of Chapter 3. Then write one word in each of these sentences.

1 Victor's young .... is dead.

2 The monster has .... him.

3 Victor has to go to .... immediately.

4 He will find the .... there.

William Is Dead

Suddenly, I stopped. There was someone behind a tree.
'No,' I thought. 'It cannot be ...' Yes! It was the monster.

Aletter from my father was waiting for me. He had terrible news. My sweet young brother William was dead!

'Last Thursday, we all went for a walk to Plainpalais,' wrote my father. 'The evening was warm and calm. William and Ernest were playing a game. Suddenly, we noticed that William was lost. We searched for him everywhere. Then we returned to the house, but he was not there. I found my dear son later, but he was dead. He was murdered! William had a small picture of your mother in his pocket, and this picture was stolen. Was this the reason for the murder? Oh,

Victor, we are all so sad! Please come home to Geneva. Elizabeth spends all day crying. Only you can help her.'

Henry watched me as I read. My happiness turned to misery. I threw the letter on the table and covered my face with my hands.

'Frankenstein!' cried Henry. 'My dear friend. What has happened?'

While Henry read the letter, I walked up and down the room.

'I must go to Geneva immediately,' I told Henry. My eyes were full of tears. 'Come with me to order the horses.'

I travelled to Geneva alone, and my journey was very sad and lonely. So many thoughts came into my mind.

'I have not been to Geneva for six years,' I said to myself, 'and a lot of things have changed.' I felt afraid but I did not know why.

The road ran by the side of Lake Geneva. I looked up at the mountains.
I loved the view, but I felt so unhappy. As I crossed the lake in a boat, a
storm began. I watched the lightning on the top of the mountains. Then the
weather got worse. I walked home through the heavy rain. It was beautiful but
frightening.

'Dear, sweet little brother William,' I thought. 'Is this storm for you?'
Suddenly I stopped. There was someone behind a tree. 'No,' I thought. 'It
cannot be ...' Yes! It was the monster! I saw him clearly when lightning lit up the
sky. I knew that it was him. It was the terrible, ugly monster that I created in
Ingoldstadt.

Why was he here? Then a thought came into my mind. Was he the murderer
of my little brother? I knew immediately that he was. I looked again for the
monster. I saw him climbing the mountain; then he disappeared in the grey
rock.

Oh, why did I create that terrible monster? I thought about my experiments. I remembered another rainy night, two years ago – the night that I gave him life. 'My own creation has murdered my brother!' I thought. Nobody can imagine my misery. I could not tell my father the true story. I could not tell anyone.

I arrived home early in the morning.

'They have found the murderer, Victor!' said my brother Ernest.

'How did they do that?' I cried. 'Nobody can follow him! It is impossible!'

Ernest did not understand what I was saying. 'The police have **arrest**ed Justine Moritz. She murdered William!'

I looked at Ernest. Justine was a sweet girl who helped Elizabeth. She worked hard and looked after William. Elizabeth was very kind to her, and everybody loved her. When my mother was dying, Justine was her nurse.

'Nobody can believe that!' I cried. 'It is wrong!'

arrest /əˈrest/ (v) to catch a possible criminal and take them to a police station

'We found the picture of Mother in her pocket. She stole it from William. That proves it, doesn't it?'

We were soon joined by Elizabeth. She was six years older too and she was more beautiful now. She welcomed me warmly, but her eyes were full of sadness.

'I do not believe that Justine is **guilty**. She is not a criminal,' said Elizabeth.

'I hope that we can prove it,' I replied.

The **trial** was the next day, and we defended Justine. But I could not say who the real criminal was. We tried to prove that Justine was not guilty. Justine did not know why the picture was in her pocket. She could not explain it. The judge did not believe her. The court decided that she was guilty. The punishment was death.

I felt very unhappy. I was **responsible** for the deaths of two people – my little brother William, and kind, sweet Justine. I was responsible for my family's pain and misery. My father and brother and Elizabeth were all suffering and I could not help them. I could not make them all happy again. And I had a terrible feeling. 'There will be more tears,' I thought. 'The monster will return.'

guilty /ˈgɪlti/ (adj) unhappy because you have done something wrong. If you are *guilty* of a crime, you did it.
trial /ˈtraɪəl/ (n) the time in a courtroom when a judge hears the facts about a person and a crime
responsible /rɪˈspɒnsəbəl/ (adj) the cause of something that has happened or of someone's actions

CHAPTER 4

Frankenstein Finds the Monster

'You made me, but now you want to destroy me.
You do not know my misery. How can you play with life like this?'

After the trial, we went back to Belrive. I liked staying there. I loved the lake. Often, at night, I waited until the rest of the family were asleep and took a boat onto the water. Sometimes I went into the middle of the lake. It was quiet and calm, and I could sit in the boat with my thoughts. My family were still crying for William. Justine was dead, and the true murderer was free. But I could not tell Elizabeth my thoughts. I was the real criminal.

I was in a state of complete misery. I knew that I was responsible. I was guilty because the monster was my creation. I wanted to find him and destroy him.

Nearly two months after the death of Justine, I decided to leave the house and travel to the mountains. I wanted to go to Chamonix. It was a place that I knew well. I often visited it when I was a boy. I went on a horse for the first part of the journey. It was the middle of August, and the weather was good. I travelled through the valley. The high mountains around me were wonderful. I loved their mystery, and the power of nature made me less afraid.

I crossed the river Arve and arrived in the valley of Chamonix. It was beautiful. There was snow on the tops of the mountains, and between the trees there were small, pretty houses. In the evening, I came to the village. Tired after my journey, I fell asleep immediately.

The next day, I decided to climb to the top of one of the mountains, Montanvert. The path was difficult and dangerous. It was raining and the sky was dark. When I arrived at the top, it was nearly midday. I sat on a rock and looked down. Below was the great glacier, like a sea of ice. Soon, the clouds disappeared and I climbed down onto the **glacier**. I spent two hours crossing it, then I stood and looked at the mountains of Mont Blanc and Montanvert. The sun came out above the clouds. The ice shone brightly.

Suddenly, I saw a man on the ice. He was quite far away, but he was coming quickly towards me. The man took long steps across the ice. Then I realized who it was. It was the monster! I was angry and I was frightened. I wanted to fight him. I wanted to kill him.

'Go away, you terrible monster!' I screamed. 'Or stay and die! I want to destroy you. But I cannot bring back the two people that you have killed!'

'Everybody hates me, and you hate me too,' replied the monster. 'But you created me. You are responsible for me. You made me, but now you want to

glacier /ˈglæsiə/ (n) a large amount of ice that moves very slowly down a mountain valley

destroy me. You do not know my misery. How can you play with life like this?
Please listen to me and help me. Do what I ask. Then I will leave you and be
good. I will never see you again. I will not make any trouble for you. And I will
not hurt anyone again. If you refuse, I will kill all your friends!

'You cannot understand how I feel,' continued the monster. 'The dark sky is much kinder to me than people are. The mountains and cold ice are my only home. You say that I am a murderer. But *you* want to murder *me*! Believe me, Frankenstein. At first, I was kind and good, but people were unkind to me. The law says that a person can defend himself. Even if he is guilty. Please listen to my story. Then you can judge me.'

3.1 Were you right?

Look back at Activity 2.4. Then read these sentences. Are they right (✓) or wrong (✗)?

1 ☐ William was murdered by Justine Moritz.

2 ☐ Victor goes home to Geneva after six years.

3 ☐ His friend Henry goes with him.

4 ☐ Victor sees the monster again after he arrives at his home.

3.2 What more did you learn?

Look at this report in a Swiss English-language newspaper. There are a number of mistakes in it. Change the words that are underlined.

MORITZ
FOUND GUILTY!

JUSTINE MORITZ

Ernest Frankenstein of Geneva was murdered last **Wednesday** near Plainpalais. Police discovered that a small picture of the boy's **sister** was stolen from his body. It was later found in the **house** of Justine Moritz, a woman who has worked in the Frankenstein house for **a few months**. The Frankenstein family were at her trial. They were **happy** when the court found her guilty. Her punishment was **twenty years in prison**.

1 ....William........

2 ....

3 ....

4 ....

5 ....

6 ....

7 ....

3.3 Language in use

Look at the sentence in the box. The first part tells us why Victor fell asleep. Write these sentences in the same way.

> **Tired after my journey,**
> I fell asleep immediately.

1 Victor studied night and day because he was very interested in science.
   Very interested in science, Victor studied night and day.

2 He forgot to eat and drink because he was busy with his experiments.
   Busy ....

3 He ran out of his laboratory because he was afraid of the monster.
   Afraid ....

4 He spent many weeks in bed because he was weak after his illness.
   Weak ....

5 He travelled into the mountains because he was crazy with misery.
   Crazy ....

6 He didn't want to listen to the monster because he was angry and afraid.
   Angry ....

3.4 What happens next?

The monster is going to tell Victor his side of the story. What do you think he will say? Tick (✓) all the answers that you think are right.

1 Everybody ...
   ☐ *is afraid of him.*
   ☐ *hates him.*
   ☐ *helps him.*
   ☐ *runs away from him.*

2 He is looking for ...
   ☐ *a friend.*
   ☐ *love.*
   ☐ *someone to kill.*
   ☐ *another monster.*
   ☐ *understanding.*

3 Victor feels ...
   ☐ *sorry.*
   ☐ *afraid.*
   ☐ *responsible.*
   ☐ *pleased.*
   ☐ *angry.*

CHAPTER 5

The Monster's Story

'More than anything, I wanted friends and I wanted love.
But I frightened people. They thought I was cruel.'

When I heard the monster's words, I felt kinder towards him. Yes, I created him. I was responsible for his happiness or unhappiness. I decided that I must listen to his story. He went across the ice, and I followed him. It started raining again. We sat down by a fire in a small hut on the mountain. The monster began to speak.

'At first I was alone and I was hungry. I took some clothes from your house, but I was cold. I do not remember very much, but I remember the forest near Ingoldstadt. I quickly learned how to live there. I ate leaves and fruit, and I drank from the river. I was not quite human, so I did not need good food. I did not know who I was. I did not know where I came from. But I learned about life. I enjoyed the song of the birds. My eyes saw light and dark – the sun in the day and the moon at night.

'Sometimes, I searched for food all day. I did not know how to make a fire. I could not get warm. One day, I saw a little hut on a hill. The door was open, so I went inside. An old man sat by the fire. He turned when he heard a noise. He looked at me and screamed. Then he ran outside, across the fields, as quickly as he could. There was some bread, milk and cheese on the table. It was the man's breakfast. I was very hungry, and I ate it quickly. I liked the hut because it was dry and warm. I fell asleep on the floor.

'Later, I continued walking across the fields. Evening came, and I arrived in a village. It seemed so wonderful! I looked at the houses and other buildings. Vegetables grew in the gardens. I went into a farmhouse. The people in there looked at me and screamed. Everyone in the village became angry. Children ran away, but men attacked me with stones. I escaped to the fields. I was frightened and unhappy.

'I found another small hut, and I went inside. I could not stand up inside it, but I slept on the floor. I was happy to find a dry place. There I could escape from the bad weather. And I could escape from the **cruel** world of people.

'I stayed in my hut. Nobody saw me there. I cleaned it and covered the holes in the walls with wood and stones. Near the hut was a pool of water. I found a cup to drink from. I had to steal food, but I was safe.

'At the side of the hut was a small house. I watched the people who lived there. Later I learned their names. There was an old man, Mr de Lacey, and

cruel /ˈkruːəl/ (adj) causing pain or sadness because you want to

his son Felix and daughter Agatha. I listened to their voices. Slowly I learned some words and began to understand their language. I found it easy to copy the sounds. At first, I only learned words like "sister", "brother", "bread" and "wood". Later, I could speak and understand more and more. I enjoyed my simple life living next to the de Laceys.

'The de Laceys came from a good family in France, but now they were quite poor. They grew vegetables in the garden, but they were often hungry. They only

had a little money for milk and bread. So I did not steal any food from them. I ate what I could find in the forest.

'Agatha was a sweet, kind young woman, and I wanted to be her friend. I thought she was beautiful and good. She made me happy. I watched Felix go into the forest every morning. He stayed there all day. When he returned, he was carrying wood for the fire. He worked very hard, so I decided to help them. At night, I went into the forest and cut wood for the family fire. I left piles of wood outside the door of the house. They were very pleased, and I enjoyed helping them. Now Felix had more time for work in his garden or repairs to the house. I tried to help them in other ways too. I swept the snow from the path. I watched Felix working, and then I did some of his work at night. They never saw me. They did know who was helping them. But they were always grateful.

'I watched the de Lacey family and learned a lot from their love and their kindness. They were beautiful and polite. Mr de Lacey went for walks with his son. Agatha often sang to her father. Their lives were simple and good.

'But I saw my face in a pool of water. They could not love me or be kind to me. I was an ugly monster. When the family went out, I went into the house. I looked at their books and slowly I learned to read. You gave me intelligence. From their books I learned about the world. I learned about different countries, about history and science. More than anything, I wanted friends and I wanted love. But I frightened people. They thought I was cruel. They thought that I wanted to hurt them.

'One day, I tried to talk to old Mr de Lacey. His eyes were very bad, and he could not see anything. "He will talk to me," I thought. "He cannot see me, so he will not judge me." I waited until Agatha and Felix were out of the house.

'I knocked at the door.

"Who is there?" said the old man.

"'Excuse me," I replied. "I am a tired traveller. Please can I sit near your fire for a few minutes?"

"'Come in," said Mr de Lacey. "You can sit here with me and rest."

"'I am alone," I told Mr de Lacey. "I have no friends. I need help, but I am afraid to ask people for it. When I meet people, they send me away. They see me as a terrible monster. But I am not a criminal."

"'I believe you," said the old man. "I can only judge your words. But how can I help you?"

'There was a noise at the entrance to the house. Felix and Agatha were coming home. It was time to speak!

"'Oh, please save me and protect me!" I cried. "I have no family or friends. Only you. I know you are kind and good. I need you ..."

"'But who are you?" cried Mr de Lacey.

'The door opened. Felix and Agatha saw me and their father together. I cannot describe their faces. They thought that I was attacking Mr de Lacey.

'When they looked at me, they started screaming. Agatha fell to the ground in fear. Felix pulled me away from his father. He picked up a stick and hit me very hard. I was in pain and very unhappy. Quickly, I escaped and went back to my hut.'

CHAPTER 6

The Monster Wants a Wife

'If I cannot have love, I will create fear.
I will take revenge on my enemy – you, Frankenstein.'

"Oh, why am I alive?" I cried to myself. I hated the person who created me. I did not want to kill myself: I was angry with the world of people, and I wanted **revenge**.

'When night came, I went into the forest. I did not try to hide now. I screamed and cried loudly. Like a wild animal, I ran through the trees and destroyed things. It was a terrible night! The stars shone in the sky, but the trees

revenge /rɪˈvendʒ/ (n) punishment for someone who has hurt you

33

had no leaves and it was cold and lonely. Everyone in the world was sleeping or happy. But I was not. I was unwanted, hated and feared by everyone.

'Soon I became tired. I lay on the ground and cried. There was not one kind person in the world. Everyone was my enemy. I hated all humans. More than anything, I hated my creator. It was time for war.

'The sun came up and I heard some men's voices. I knew that I could not go back to my hut. So I hid myself in some trees. I spent the day thinking, "What shall I do? Where shall I go?"

'I felt calmer in the warm sun and clean air. I fell asleep, but I had bad dreams. When I woke up, it was night. I was hungry. I found some food to eat. Then I went back to my little hut and stayed there quietly. Morning came, but the family were not there. The inside of the house was dark and silent.

'Soon Felix came along the path with two other men.

'"It is impossible," he said. "We cannot live here now. My father's life is in danger. My sister will never forget what we saw. We must leave this place."

'He went inside for a few minutes. Then he left. I never saw anyone from the de Lacey family again.

'I stayed in my hut for the rest of the day. I was sad and angry, and I wanted revenge. My friends, the de Laceys, were gone. Now I had nothing. I did not belong to the world. I started thinking about death. I remembered my friends' kind faces and I felt calmer. Then my anger came back. I was alone and I could not take revenge on them. So I decided to destroy the house.

'I waited until night time. There was a strong wind, and the clouds disappeared from the sky. I lit a dry piece of wood and danced angrily around the house. Then I pushed the burning wood into the wall. The house burned quickly. I watched the orange and yellow fire destroy the de Laceys' home, then I ran as far away as possible.

'I decided to find you, Frankenstein. You created me. You were responsible for me. When I left your laboratory, I took a piece of paper with me. It had your name on it. I knew the names of towns from the de Laceys' conversations and from their books. I discovered that you were in Geneva. So I went after you. I had to follow the sun, because I had no map. I felt only hate towards you, but I wanted you to help me. You gave me a heart with feelings, and then you sent me into the cruel world. You also made me an ugly monster that humans hated and feared.

'It was late in the autumn when I left. There was no sun. Rain and snow fell around me. The rivers were frozen, and the earth was hard and cold. I only travelled at night. I did not want to meet anyone. I suffered a lot. My heart grew cold and hard. I thought only of revenge.

'After a long time, I arrived in Geneva. It was spring, and the world was green again. In the evening, I found a hiding place in some fields. I felt terrible because I was so hungry and tired. I was falling asleep when a noise woke me. It was the sound of a child who ran into my field. Suddenly, I had an idea. This child was

young. He did not have fear or hate in his heart. "I will take him and talk to him," I thought. "He will not hate me because I am ugly. I will make him my friend. Then I will not be so lonely in this world."

'So I pulled the boy towards me. When he looked at me, he screamed in fear.

"'Child," I said. "I will not hurt you. Listen to me."

"'Stop!" the boy cried. "You are a monster! You want to eat me! Stop, or I will tell my father!"

"'Boy, you will never see your father again. You must come with me."

"'Ugly monster, go away! My father is Mr Frankenstein. He will punish you."

"'Frankenstein! So you belong to my enemy. Now I can have my revenge."

'The child fought me and tried to escape. But I put my hands around his neck, and in a few minutes he was dead. I looked at the body that lay on the ground. My hands left black **mark**s on his neck. My heart felt happy and proud.

"'Frankenstein will know suffering too now!" I said to myself.

mark /mɑːk/ (n) a small dark area or cut on something

'Then I noticed a small picture in the child's pocket. I looked at it. It was a beautiful woman. This made me angrier. A beautiful woman could never love me. I took the picture and walked to a hut in the field. I wanted somewhere to hide. In the hut, a young woman was sleeping. I watched her. She must not wake up and see me. Then I had an idea. I put the small picture in the pocket of her dress. "They will think that she is the murderer," I thought. Then I ran away as fast as I could.

'So, Frankenstein,' the monster said, 'that is my story. I came to these mountains, hoping to find you. You must not go until you have promised me something. I am alone. My life is misery, and humans will never be my friend. So I want you to create another monster. I want a wife.'

The monster finished speaking. He looked at me carefully, waiting for my reply. I was very surprised. I did not know what to say. Then he continued.

'You must create a female for me, as ugly and terrible as I am. I will be able to live with her and have a friend. Only you can do this. Then I will not be lonely and unhappy. You are responsible for me, and you cannot refuse.'

'I do refuse,' I shouted. 'Shall I create another monster like you? Then two **evil** monsters will live in the world. Go away! You can do what you want to me. I will never agree.'

'You are wrong,' answered the monster. 'And I will explain. I am bad because I am unhappy. I am hated by everyone. There is no reason for me to like humans. They do not like me. If I cannot have love, I will create fear. I will take revenge on my enemy – you, Frankenstein.' The monster looked very angry when he spoke. 'But if you agree, I promise to leave you alone. We will go far away and live in the forests of South America.

'I do not eat the same food as humans. I do not kill animals for food. I only eat leaves and fruit. My wife will be the same as me. We will sleep on a bed of dry leaves. We will live quietly, and you will never see us again.'

I listened to the monster's words. I understood him better now. I was not so angry and afraid. Perhaps he was right. The monster showed that he had deep feelings. I, his creator, had the power to give him happiness.

'Do you promise that you will never return to Europe? Do you promise that you will never hurt anyone again?' I asked.

'Yes,' cried the monster. 'I promise.'

'Then I agree to your request.'

'Go and start work, and I will wait. When she is ready, I will come back to you.'

With these words, the monster disappeared across the ice.

evil /ˈiːvəl/ (n/adj) something that is very, very bad

4.1 Were you right?

Look back at Activity 3.4. Then read the sentences below. Are they right (✓) or wrong (✗)?

1 ☐ The monster does not steal food from poor people.
2 ☐ The monster secretly does work for the de Lacey family.
3 ☐ Old Mr de Lacey is afraid when he sees the monster.
4 ☐ The monster burns the de Laceys' hut with them inside it.
5 ☐ The monster killed William and put the picture in Justine's pocket.
6 ☐ The monster promises to leave Europe for ever if Victor helps him.
7 ☐ Victor refuses to make a female monster.

4.2 What more did you learn?

Who says, or thinks, these words? Match the sentences to the pictures and write their names.

1 'Look, sister. Someone has cut some wood and put it outside our door. How strange!'
...... Felix de Lacey ......

2 'I can't see you, but your voice sounds sad. I'll help you if I can.'
....

3 'I'll never forget what I saw, Felix. We can't continue living in this hut now.'
....

4 'I don't eat meat – only fruit and leaves. I can live in the forest, far away from people.'
....

5 'I'm sorry for you and I feel responsible for you. Perhaps now I can make you happy.'
....

4.3 Language in use

Look at the sentence in the box. Then complete the sentences below. What happens after the monster arrives near Ingoldstadt?

'I **am hated** by everyone.'

1   The monster steals villagers' food.
    The villagers' food is stolen (by the monster).

2   The monster helps the de Laceys in many ways.
    ....

3   He cuts their wood.
    ....

4   He sweeps the snow from their path.
    ....

5   He also watches them all the time.
    ....

6   Finally, Felix hits the monster and sends him away.
    ....

4.4 What happens next?

What do you think? Complete the table.

	Who promises?	Will the promise be kept?
I promise I will go to South America.		
I promise I will make you a wife.		

CHAPTER 7

Frankenstein in England

*I felt nervous because the monster was waiting. 'He will be angry,'
I thought, 'if his wife is not ready soon.'*

I left Chamonix and returned to Geneva. I was nervous and frightened. My meeting with the monster was a very unpleasant memory. And now I had to make another monster. What a terrible promise!

Days passed. I did not feel brave enough to start my work. I was afraid of the monster's revenge. I could not make a female without more scientific information. I knew that I had to go to England. I needed to visit some scientists there. There I could do some more experiments and start work on the new monster.

My health was much better now. When I was able to forget about my promise, I felt happy. I tried to enjoy myself. I went out on the lake in my boat. The sun and fresh air calmed me. My father noticed that I was happier.

One day, he spoke to me about an important subject.

'My dear son, I have always hoped that you and Elizabeth will marry. You have been friends since you were children. You studied together. You like the same things. I believe that you will be happy together. Do you love her only as a sister? Or do you hope that she will be your wife? Tell me, Victor, have you given your heart to another woman?'

'My dear father,' I replied, 'I love my cousin very much. She is the loveliest and most interesting woman that I have ever known. I want to marry her. The marriage will bring future happiness for all of us.'

My father was pleased. 'I am very glad to hear you say this, Victor. When you marry, this will become a happy home again. You are young and have enough money. Do you want to marry now? Or do you have any other plans?'

I listened to my father in silence. I waited before I answered him. I could not marry Elizabeth yet! The thought filled me with **horror** and misery. I had to keep a terrible promise. I had to make the female monster. Then the two monsters could go away together. Elizabeth and I had to wait for our happiness.

I also had to travel. I wanted to learn from the work of the English scientists, and I did not want to create the monster in my father's house. So I told him that I wanted to travel and study for a few months. When I returned, I wanted to marry Elizabeth.

My father thought that travelling was a good idea. My health was better, but I needed a holiday. So he did not refuse my request. He and Elizabeth suggested

horror /ˈhɒrə/ (n) a strong feeling of fear caused by something very unpleasant

that Henry joined me. I agreed to start my journey with my friend. Henry was amusing, and I enjoyed spending time with him. But I wanted to be alone when I started my work. I did not want Henry to meet the monster.

Henry and I agreed on our holiday plans. I prepared for my journey. Elizabeth was sad and she worried about me. She wanted me to return quickly. When she said goodbye, there were tears in her eyes.

I travelled to Strasbourg and waited there for Henry. After two days, he arrived, and we left together. He was happy and amused by everything that he saw. But I had unhappy thoughts and did not notice the beautiful country around me. I thought about the horror of the monster and the work that I had to do. It was impossible to enjoy myself.

We travelled along the river Rhine and passed beautiful towns and villages. Henry pointed to all the mountains and lakes on the journey. He was excited by everything. My good friend was full of love for life!

We travelled through Holland, to Rotterdam, and took a ship to England. On a clear day in December, I first saw the white coast of Britain. On the way to London, we passed through places that we knew from English history. At last, Henry and I arrived in that famous city.

We decided to stay in London for a few months. It was a wonderful, interesting place. Henry wanted to learn as much as he could. I wanted to talk to the scientists who worked there. I wanted to enjoy our visit, but one thing was always in my mind – my promise to the monster. I tried to hide my misery from my friend much as possible. I did not want him to worry about me. I often refused to go out with him. I told him that I was busy. I had to be alone. I began to collect the things that I needed for the monster. I hated thinking about the job. I hated every minute that I spent on it. But I had to continue.

After a few months in London, we were invited to visit Scotland. We both wanted to go, but I did not want to meet a lot of people. I wanted to leave the city and see mountains and lakes. It was now February. We decided to make a journey through England and to arrive in Scotland at the end of July. I took my chemistry equipment and the things that I needed. I decided to find a quiet place in the north of Scotland. I could finish my work there.

We left London in March, and visited Windsor and Oxford. I enjoyed these famous old cities. I remembered my own past with sadness. When I was young, I was never unhappy. Everything interested me. Now, I was like a tree that was hit by lightning. I was very different now.

After some time, we moved north. We visited the Lake District* in the north of England. It was wonderful, like our own country, with its beautiful mountains and lakes.

'I would like to spend my life here and forget Switzerland!' cried Henry.

But I remembered my promise. I felt nervous because the monster was waiting. 'He will be angry,' I thought, 'if his wife is not ready soon.' I lived in fear. The monster knew where my family lived. He could kill them at any time.

When we arrived in Scotland, we visited Edinburgh for a week. Our friend lived in the city of Perth. He was waiting for us to arrive. But I did not want to laugh and talk with other people. I wanted to continue without Henry. 'Please enjoy yourself, Henry,' I said. 'I would like to be alone. I will be happier when I return.'

Henry sadly agreed, and I promised to write to him often. I went to the north of Scotland. I wanted to be as far away as I could from people. I felt sure that the monster was following me. 'When the female is ready, he will visit me,' I thought.

I found a small island in the Orkneys.* This was a good place to create my terrible monster. The island was like a large rock with a few huts on it. Nothing grew there. It was not pleasant or friendly. I had to get food from a larger island, five miles away. I stayed in one of the huts. It had two rooms, and one of them became my laboratory.

In the mornings, I worked. In the evenings, I walked on the stony beach. It was a cold, lonely place. My work became more and more difficult. My heart felt sick when I looked at my equipment and the body parts for the female monster. But soon I hoped to finish my job and leave that terrible, lonely island.

* The Lake District: an area in the north-west of England. There are beautiful lakes and mountains there. It is popular for walking holidays.

* The Orkneys: a group of islands to the north of Scotland. They are quite far away from the coast.

CHAPTER 8

Another Murder

'Who will he murder next?' I asked myself.
I remembered his words: 'I will be with you on your wedding night.'

I sat in my laboratory one evening. The moon was shining over the sea, but I did not have enough light for my work. I thought about my life – and my work. My brother was murdered by my own creation. The monster murdered my brother. And now I was creating another monster.

'Will she be worse than her husband?' I thought. 'Will she enjoy being cruel? Will they go away to the forests of South America? He has promised. But what will happen if the female refuses? What will he do if she does not love him? Will she hate the monster because he is ugly? Will she prefer a handsome man and leave him? What will he do then, when he is unhappy again?

'Or will the monster want to have children? Imagine a family of monsters! I cannot be responsible for that danger to the world!

'How can I create this female monster?' I asked myself. 'It is a crazy, terrible thing to do. I cannot do it. The world will never forgive me!'

I was shaking with fear. I looked up. By the light of the moon, I saw the monster. He was standing by the window with a terrible smile on his face. Yes, he was following me. He was waiting in the forests, hiding in the mountains and sleeping in fields. He was watching me. He was there for his female.

I looked at him. His face was evil and cruel. I thought about my promise. I knew that I could not create another monster like him. I destroyed the body on the table.

The monster saw me destroy his future happiness. With an angry scream, he disappeared from the window. I left the room and locked the door. In my bedroom, I was alone with my thoughts. I was very frightened.

Many hours passed. I stayed near the window and looked out at the sea. It was a calm night. The quiet moon looked down on the water. I saw some boats, but everything was silent. Suddenly, I heard a boat arrive at the beach. Someone was walking towards my hut. I knew that it was the monster. Nobody could help me. It was like a terrible dream. I could not move. Soon I heard the monster's steps outside. He opened the door and came in.

'You have destroyed the work which you began. Why did you do that? Are you going to break your promise? I have waited for a long time. I left Switzerland with you. I followed you through the hills and mountains and fields of England and Scotland. Do you think that it was an easy journey? I have been very tired, and hungry, and cold. Why are you destroying all my hopes?'

'Go away! Yes, I am breaking my promise. I will never create another monster like you,' I replied.

'Remember that I have power,' said the monster. 'You believe that you are unhappy now. But I can bring you more misery. Then you will not want to live. You created me, but I have power too. Do what I tell you!'

'You have power. But I will not do something that I know is wrong. If you do not have a wife, you cannot do bad things together. Should I make another monster like you? A monster who enjoys death and misery?'

The monster looked at me angrily. 'Every man has a wife; every animal has a female! Why do I have to be alone? Be careful, Frankenstein! You will never be happy again. I will have my revenge! You can destroy my dreams and hopes, but revenge will be more important to me than light or food! I will die, but first you will be sorry! Remember, I have no fear, and so I have power. I will watch you. You will be sorry!'

'Stop!' I cried. 'You cannot change my mind.'

'I will leave. But remember this: I will be with you on your wedding night.'

Everything was silent again, but I heard the monster's words in my head. I was very angry. I wanted to throw him into the ocean and kill him. I walked up and down my room. 'Why did I not follow him? I should fight him until one of us is dead,' I thought. But he was not on the island now. I was afraid of his revenge. 'Who will he murder next?' I asked myself. I remembered his words: *I will be with you on your wedding night.*

I imagined the monster's plan. 'He is going to kill me on my wedding night,' I thought. 'Then he will have his revenge.' I was not afraid to die, but I thought of my dear Elizabeth. I thought of her crying sadly after my death. Tears poured from my eyes. I knew that I must be strong. 'I will not let my enemy destroy me. Not without a fight,' I decided.

The night passed, and the sun came up. I felt calmer. I left the house and walked on the beach. The sea was like a wall between me and the rest of the world. It protected me. I wanted to stay on that rock forever. I told myself, 'If I go back to the world, the monster will kill me. Or he will kill the people that I love.' But I was his creator and I had to do something.

I sat on the beach all day. Then a boat arrived and brought me some letters. Some were from Geneva. One was from Henry, asking me to join him again in Perth. He was bored and wanted to see me. Then we could travel south to London together. I decided to leave in two days.

First, I had to go back to my laboratory and put all my equipment away. This was not a pleasant job. I had to touch all the tools that I now hated. So the next day I opened the door. I cleaned and put away the chemistry equipment. The half-finished monster lay in pieces on the floor. I did not want the local people to discover the body, so I put the pieces into a bag with a lot of stones. I decided to throw the bag into the sea.

At three o'clock in the morning, I got in a boat and sailed a few miles out. It was very dark and I threw my bag into the water. Nobody saw me.

I enjoyed sailing on the water. I decided not to return immediately. I lay in the bottom of the boat and soon fell asleep.

I do not know how long I was asleep. But the sun was high in the sky when I woke up. The wind was in the north-east. I was far away from the island. But I did not know which way to sail the boat. I was lost on the water and I was very thirsty. I imagined my death at sea. I thought of the unhappiness of Elizabeth, of my father and of Henry. 'Monster!' I cried. 'You will have your revenge.'

The boat continued to move for a few more hours. I was very tired and frightened. I did not know where I was going. Suddenly, I saw some land. I cried with happiness.

When I came nearer to the coast, I saw some ships. There was a town near the beach. I was tired and dirty and untidy, but I had money with me. I could buy some food and drink. I arrived at the coast and got out of my small boat. A crowd of people were waiting for me.

I spoke to them in English. 'Good friends,' I asked. 'Please can you tell me where I am? What is the name of this town?'

'You will know that very soon,' replied a man with a deep voice. 'But you will not like it here. You will not sleep in a hotel tonight. I can tell you that.'

'Why are you so rude?' I asked.

'We do not like criminals in Ireland,' said the man.

More people arrived. They looked at me strangely.

'You must come to Mr Kirwin's,' said another man.

'Who is Mr Kirwin?' I asked.

'A man was found dead here last night. I am arresting you,' the man said. 'For murder.'

5.1 Were you right?

Look back at Activity 4.4. Then circle the right ending to each sentence.

1 Victor cannot marry Elizabeth
   a until he has made a female monster. **b** until his health is better.

2 Victor travels to England
   a to talk to scientists there. **b** to get away from the monster.

3 Victor goes to a small, lonely island in the Orkneys
   a to get far away from people. **b** to get away from the monster.

4 Victor starts work on a female monster,
   a but he can't give it life. **b** but he destroys it.

5.2 What more did you learn?

Number these in the right order, 1–10.

a `1` Victor agrees to marry Elizabeth.

b ☐ Victor puts together the parts for a female monster.

c ☐ Victor is arrested for murder.

d ☐ The monster promises to have revenge on Victor.

e ☐ The monster arrives on Victor's island.

f ☐ Victor leaves Henry in Perth.

g ☐ Victor throws the parts of his female monster into the sea.

h ☐ Victor and Henry enjoy the Lake District.

i ☐ Victor gets lost on the sea.

j ☐ Henry and Victor arrive in London.

Orkneys

SCOTLAND

Perth

Edinburgh

Lake District

ENGLAND

WALES

Oxford

London

Windsor

5.3 Language in use

Look at the sentences in the box. Then make similar sentences. Use one of these words in each sentence:

> I wanted to talk to the scientists **who** lived there.
>
> I had to touch all the tools **that** I now hated.

| who | that | where |

1 Victor thought about his work. He had to do it.
Victor thought about the work that he had to do.

2 He and Henry passed through some famous places. They knew about those places from books.

....

3 Henry is an old friend. Victor has known him for many years.

....

4 Victor found a place in the Orkneys. He could finish his work there.

....

5 He has created a monster. The monster enjoys death and misery.

....

6 Victor found the body parts. He needed them.

....

5.4 What happens next?

Victor is in prison in Ireland for murder! Look at the picture on pages 54 and 55. What do you think? Make notes.

Notes
Who is dead?

Who has killed the dead person?

How does Victor feel?

Will the Irish judge find Victor guilty of murder?

CHAPTER 9

Frankenstein in Prison

I could not do anything or go anywhere.
I had to stay in the prison, waiting for the trial.

I was taken immediately to see Mr Kirwin, the local judge. He was a kind old man, but he looked at me seriously. He told some men to come into the room. He asked one of them to describe what happened last night.

'I was on my boat with my son, catching fish. It was very windy, and so we returned to the coast. We walked along the beach. Then we saw the body of a man on the ground. Dead. He was a handsome young man of about twenty-five

years old. There was no sign of a fight, but there were black marks around his neck. The killer was very strong.'

I listened nervously. The monster! I had to sit down because I was shaking with fear.

'Then we saw a boat. There was only one man in it. He was not far from the coast,' the man said. He looked at me strangely.

The judge asked some other people to tell their story. They all saw a man in a boat – but I was still on the island at that time. Mr Kirwin took me into a room where the body lay. How can I describe the horror that I felt? I saw my dear friend Henry Clerval lying dead in front of me. I threw myself on the body and cried.

'Has my terrible work killed you too, my dearest Henry? I have already destroyed two people. But you, Henry, my friend ...'

Two men carried me out of the room. I screamed and cried and became very ill.

◆

For two months I lay in bed, near to death. During my illness, I had terrible dreams and talked like a crazy person. I asked people to help me destroy the monster. I was, said I, the murderer of Justine, William and Henry. I thought that I could feel the monster's fingers on my neck. I screamed loudly. I felt great fear and sadness. 'I hope that I will die,' I thought.

When I woke up, I was in a dark room in prison. I looked around and saw bars on the window. Then I remembered everything. It was not a dream. It was real horror and pain. I could not do anything or go anywhere. I had to stay in the prison, waiting for the trial.

Mr Kirwin came to see me. He was interested in me and wanted to help me. 'Are you comfortable? Is there anything that I can do for you?' he asked.

'Thank you, but there is nothing in the world that can help me,' I replied.

'I know that you are far from home. You arrived in this country and were arrested for murder. I was there when you saw the body of your friend. I believe that you are not guilty.'

'It does not matter to me,' I replied sadly. 'Death will not be unwelcome.'

'When you became ill, I looked at your papers. I found some letters. One was from your father. I wrote to him, and he has come to visit you.'

A few minutes later, my father came into the room. I was very pleased to see him and held out my hand to him.

'You are safe, father – and Elizabeth – and Ernest?'

My father calmed me.

'The family are well,' he told me. 'A prison is not a happy place, my son. And poor Clerval ... '

The name of my friend brought tears to my eyes. I was still quite ill and weak. But my father looked after me and I slowly got better. He believed that my illness was an illness of the mind. I did not explain, or tell him about the monster. I was always silent about that. 'People will think I am crazy,' I thought. But the story was too frightening to tell.

I stayed in prison for three months. Then we went to the court for the trial. At the trial, the judge believed my story. I was on the Orkney Islands when Henry's body was found. This proved that I was not guilty. I was free to leave prison at last.

CHAPTER 10

Back in Switzerland

'I have a terrible secret that I must tell you.
When you hear it, you will look at me in horror.'

My father and I started our journey home to Switzerland. When we arrived in Paris, I was very tired. I needed to rest before we continued. I did not want to meet people or talk to anybody. My father could not understand that.

'Justine was not guilty of murder,' I said to him. 'But she died. I murdered her. William, Justine and Henry – they all died because of me.'

'My dear son,' replied my father with surprise. 'Please do not talk like this! You are imagining all these terrible things.'

'No father, I am not crazy. It is true. They were not guilty, but my work has killed them.'

My father thought that I was still not well. He changed the subject of our conversation. He never spoke about Ireland again, or about what happened there.

As time passed, I felt calmer. I hated myself, and was sorry for everything. But I did not talk about my crimes again. I stayed calm and silent.

A few days before we left Paris, a letter arrived. It was from Elizabeth.

My dear friend

I was very pleased to receive a letter from my uncle, from Paris. You are not very far away now. I hope to see you in less than two weeks. My poor cousin, you have suffered so much! I have been very worried about you. But I hope that you are completely well now.

I do not want you to worry about anything. But I want to ask you a question.

Since we were children, your parents have wanted us to marry. We have always been good friends, but perhaps this is enough for you. Tell me, dearest Victor, do you love another woman?

You have travelled a lot and spent a long time at Ingoldstadt. When I saw you last year, you looked very unhappy. You wanted to be alone. I guessed that you did not want to marry me. Are you sorry about the promise that you made to your mother? And are you worried about your father's unhappiness if the marriage does not happen?

Victor, I must tell you that I love you. In my dreams of the future, you are my husband. But I do not only want my happiness – I want your happiness too. I cannot marry you if it will make you unhappy. You must be free to choose. If you are happy, I will not be lonely or sad.

Do not answer this letter if it is painful. My uncle will send me news of your health, and we will meet soon. I hope that you will have a smile on your face. Then I will not need any other happiness.
Elizabeth Lavenza

I read the letter. Then I remembered the monster's words: *'I will be with you on your wedding night.'* He wanted to take away my only hope of happiness. He planned to kill me. 'There will be a fight between us,' I thought. 'If the monster wins, I will be dead. He will have no more power over me. But if I destroy him, I will be free at last. Then I can be happy with Elizabeth.'

Sweet, lovely Elizabeth. I read the letter again and again. I dreamed of love. I decided that we must marry very soon. 'If I wait, the monster will take revenge in another way,' I thought. I wrote a letter to Elizabeth.

'Do not be afraid,' I wrote. 'I love only you. I promise that I will try to bring you happiness. But I have a terrible secret that I must tell you. When you hear it,

you will look at me in horror. I will tell you my story of misery the day after our marriage, because, my sweet cousin, there must be no secrets between us. But until then, I will say nothing more about this subject.'

We returned to Geneva a week later. Elizabeth welcomed me, but there were tears in her eyes. I was not the same person. I was thin after my long illness. She was different too. She was thinner, and her face was not as bright and happy as before. But she was warm and kind. I needed her calmness and sweetness.

My father spoke to me about the wedding.

'Do you love another woman?' he asked.

'No. Only Elizabeth. Let's decide on a date for the wedding. I promise that, in life or in death, I will give myself to her.'

When I thought about the monster, I felt terrible. There were days when I did not speak to anybody. I was angry and crazy. Elizabeth was the only person who could help me. Her quiet voice calmed me. But the monster's words were in my ears: *'I will be with you on your wedding night.'*

6.1 Were you right?

Look back at your notes in Activity 5.4. Then circle the right answers below.

1 The monster has killed *Henry Clervil / Mr Kirwin / a fisherman*.

2 Victor was in prison for three *days / weeks / months*.

3 *Elizabeth / His father / His brother* visits him in prison.

4 Victor wants to marry Elizabeth but he is afraid of *her father / his father / the monster*.

6.2 What more did you learn?

What are these people thinking? Write the correct letters.

A 'I want to marry him, but does he love me?'

B 'I want to marry him, but my father is against it.'

C 'I know he loves me. But I can't marry him.'

A 'I want to marry her, but not for two or three years.'

B 'I want to marry her, but I'm afraid. What will the monster do?

C 'She loves me, but I can't marry her.'

A 'I don't know why his father came here.'

B 'I'm sure this young man is guilty of murder.'

C 'I don't think he killed his friend.'

A 'I think he is crazy and ill. I want to take him home.'

B 'This judge is not very helpful.'

C 'He is not pleased to see me. I think he hates me.'

6.3 Language in use

Look at the sentence in the box, an answer to Victor's question in the picture. Complete other answers to his question. Use these words.

> I **have** already **destroyed** two people.

| throw | destroy | see | create | make | murder | promise | break |

1 I ....*have created*.... a terrible monster.

2 This monster .... my brother and my friend.

3 I .... my promise to the monster.

4 I .... the female monster.

5 I .... the pieces into the sea.

6 This .... the monster very angry.

7 He .... to be at my wedding.

8 I .... the terrible things that this monster can do.

> What have I done?

6.4 What happens next?

How do you think the story will end? Make notes in answer to these questions.

Notes

Will Victor marry Elizabeth?

Will they live happily together?

Will the monster kill again? (Who?)

Will Victor kill the monster or will the monster kill Victor?

CHAPTER 11

Elizabeth

Suddenly, I heard a loud scream. It came from Elizabeth's room.
Then, of course, I understood the monster's plan!

Everyone prepared for the wedding. We all tried to be happy. Relatives and friends came to visit us. I laughed and smiled. We planned to have a quiet holiday after the wedding. My father thought that I was happy. But Elizabeth knew that something was wrong. I had a secret to tell her. But also, I was preparing for my own death.

I looked around for the monster everywhere I went. I carried a gun with me. But I felt safer and calmer as the day of our marriage came closer.

Elizabeth seemed shy and quiet on the wedding day. My father did not think that this was strange. She was just a young woman who was getting married. But I could see that she was worried. Perhaps she knew that danger was near.

After the wedding, there was a large party. Then Elizabeth and I said goodbye to everyone and began our holiday. It was a lovely day. Everyone smiled as we left. We started our journey by water. We planned to stay the night at a hotel, and continue our journey the next day.

That was the last happy day of my life. The sun was hot, and we enjoyed the beautiful country. The wonderful mountains were high above us, at the side of the lake.

I took Elizabeth's hand. 'You are sad, my love! You do not know what I have suffered. But let's enjoy this beautiful day together and not be sad.'

'Be happy, dear Victor,' replied Elizabeth. 'Do not worry, my heart is not sad. Something tells me that I must not be too happy. But I will not listen to that terrible voice. Look at the pretty clouds above Mont Blanc. Look at the fish in the clear water of the lake. It is a wonderful day! Look! Everything in the world is happy today!'

We watched the sun go down over the lake. There was a light, warm wind over the water. It moved softly through the trees, and we could smell beautiful flowers. But when we arrived at the side of the lake, my fears about the monster returned.

It was eight o'clock when the boat arrived. We walked for a short time near the lake. It was getting dark, and the mountains were black against the sky. We enjoyed the dying light, and then went to the hotel.

The wind was stronger now, and the moon was in the sky. The water on the lake became rougher. Suddenly, it started to rain. There was a bad storm.

As night came, a thousand fears came into my mind. I was nervous. I looked

all around me for the monster. I knew that he was there somewhere. He was waiting to kill me. I jumped every time that I heard a sound. But I decided to fight my enemy. I could not run away from him. 'I must fight until one of us is dead,' I said to myself.

Elizabeth watched me. 'What is it, my dear Victor?' she asked. 'What are you afraid of?'

'Everything will be safe, after tonight,' I replied. 'But tonight will be terrible.'

I watched and waited like this for an hour. Then I realized that it was very unpleasant for Elizabeth. I suggested that she went to bed. I did not want to join her yet. I wanted to find out where the monster was hiding.

Elizabeth left me and went to the bedroom. I walked up and down the hotel. I looked for the monster everywhere, but I could not find him. Suddenly, I heard a loud scream. It came from Elizabeth's room. Then, of course, I understood the monster's plan! A second later, the scream was repeated. I ran into the room.

Oh, why did I not die then and there? Why did I live to tell this horror story? Elizabeth was lying across the bed – dead. Her head hung down and her hair covered her face. She was murdered, on her wedding night. I fell to the floor. For a few minutes I could remember nothing.

When I opened my eyes, people from the hotel were standing around me. There was horror in their eyes. I ran back to the bed where Elizabeth lay. Somebody had moved her body, and she seemed to be asleep. I held her in my arms and kissed her, but her skin was cold and she was not breathing. The marks of the monster's evil hands were on her neck.

I looked up for a minute. The window was open, and the yellow light of the moon shone into the room. Then I saw him. He stood outside with a terrible, ugly smile on his face. He seemed to laugh as he pointed towards Elizabeth's body. I ran to the window and pulled out my gun. I shot at him, but he moved quickly and escaped. He ran away very fast and jumped into the lake.

When they heard the sound of the gun, a large group of people came into the room. I pointed outside and everybody came with me to the lake. We followed the monster's path, but he was gone.

After a few hours, we returned. People searched around the lake, but they found nothing. Nobody saw the monster. They believed that I was imagining him.

We searched the forest next, but I became weak and ill. Some people had to carry me back to the hotel. I was put on a bed. I looked around the room, but I could not think clearly about anything. I was too unhappy.

After a short time, I got up. I went to the room where Elizabeth lay. Women were standing by the bed, crying. I started to cry too. I was responsible for the deaths of William, Justine, Henry, and now Elizabeth – my wife for only a few hours. But were my father and brother safe? Perhaps the monster planned to kill them too. This idea made me scream with fear. I decided to return to Geneva as fast as possible.

I could not get any horses that night, so I had to travel across the lake. There was still a storm, and the rain was heavy. Two men sailed the boat for me. I felt too sick to do it myself. My arms were not strong enough. I rested my head in my hands. Just yesterday, Elizabeth and I were on this lake together. Now she was dead. Her life was a memory. Tears poured down my face.

All my future happiness was gone – stolen by the monster. A monster that I created. Nobody has ever been as unhappy as me, in the history of the world.

I arrived in Geneva. My father and brother Ernest were still alive. I had to tell them about Elizabeth. My father heard the news, but it was too terrible for him. I can see him now – an excellent and kind old man. His eyes lost their brightness. His Elizabeth was dead! He could not live with this new horror. He could not get out of his bed, and a few days later he died in my arms.

CHAPTER 12

The End of the Monster

I moved towards the sound of his voice,
but he disappeared into the dark shadows.

What happened to me? After my father died, I could not do anything. Sometimes I dreamed about my younger days. I was walking in lovely green fields with my friends. Then I woke up, and I was alone. I was in a small, dark room. I thought it was a prison. But it was a hospital. People thought that I was crazy. So I was kept alone in a small room in the hospital for many months.

I thought about the monster. He was still free, somewhere in the world. I wanted to find him. I needed my revenge.

I went to the police. 'I know who my wife's murderer is. I know who has destroyed my family,' I told them.

'Do not worry, Mr Frankenstein,' the judge said in a kind voice. 'We will try to find the murderer. We will do everything that we can.'

'Please listen to my story,' I said. 'It is very strange, but it is all true.' I then told him about the monster. I told him all the facts in a calm voice.

The judge listened to me. At first, he seemed surprised but interested. Then he looked at me in horror. I thought that he did not believe me.

'I want to help you,' he said slowly, after I finished my story. 'But this monster is stronger and more powerful than a human. We cannot follow him across glaciers and mountains. It is impossible! And we do not know where he has gone now. The murder happened a few months ago.'

'I am sure that he is near my house,' I replied. 'If he is in the mountains, you can search for him like an animal. But I see that you do not believe me.'

'If we find this monster, then we will arrest him for his crimes,' the judge said. 'But I am afraid that it will be difficult to find him.'

'Then I must look for him alone. I will not rest until I find the monster. I will spend the rest of my life looking for him. You cannot understand my feelings. I created this monster, and he still exists. I must destroy him.'

My face was red with anger while I spoke. The judge looked at me. He thought that I was crazy. So he spoke to me kindly, like a nurse to a child. I became angrier and ran from his office.

I decided to leave Geneva. When I was happy, it was a beautiful place. But now I hated it. I took some money and left. I had to look for the monster. William, Elizabeth and my father were dead, but I was still alive. I had to continue living to destroy the monster. He knew where I was. But I did not know where he was.

One night I heard him. I was outside in the woods when I heard a cruel laugh. He spoke to me. 'I am happy, Frankenstein. You are still alive, so I am happy!'

I moved towards the sound of his voice, but he disappeared into the dark shadows.

So this is my story. For many months, I have followed the monster. I have been all over Europe. He knows that I am following him. But I can never catch him. Sometimes he leaves me messages. He writes on stone, or on the side of a tree. His messages are cruel:

Follow me! I will take you to a country of ice, in the far north of the world.
You will feel the misery of the cold. But I am not human – I do not feel it.
You are my enemy and I want you to suffer.

Now it is winter, and it is very cold. I have followed the monster to these glaciers. I have had to look for food under the ice. The monster is going

farther and farther north. It is very difficult to travel through the snow and ice, even with dogs. I hate life now. I prefer to sleep, because in my dreams I see my old friends.

One day, I arrived in a village. The people there were talking about a terrible, ugly monster. He was carrying guns, and frightened everybody. He stole all their food. I was very angry to hear this. The monster has escaped from me again and again. But I must continue my slow journey across the ocean of ice.

When I saw your ship, Walton, I wanted to ask for your help. I wanted a boat to continue my journey to the top of the world. I need to find my enemy and destroy him. But I am tired and weak. I am dying and I cannot continue.

Death will be welcome, but the monster is still alive! If I die, Walton, will you look for him? I want revenge! He will come here after I am dead. Will you promise to destroy the evil monster?

The Last Letter

'Oh, Frankenstein,' cried the monster, 'will you forgive me?
But you cannot answer me ...'

M y dear sister Margaret
You have probably finished reading my friend's terrible story now. It is the saddest, strangest and most frightening story that I have ever heard. But I must tell you now what happened next.

For some time, the ship was in danger in the thick ice. The men on the ship were afraid of dying far away from home. Frankenstein lay, very ill, in bed.

'My men want me to return,' I told him. 'I cannot take them into more danger. I must return to England. I had a dream, and I do not want to fail. But my men's lives are more important than the North Pole.'

'I will not return with you,' he replied. 'I must stay here and find the monster.'

He tried to get up, but he was not strong enough. He fell back in his bed and closed his eyes.

I sat by the bed and watched him. I thought that he was sleeping. After a few hours, he opened his eyes and spoke to me in a quiet, weak voice.

'I am going to die, Walton,' he said. 'I want revenge and I want to see the end of the monster. The monster was cruel and evil. He destroyed my brother, my best friend, and my wife. I am afraid that he will kill more people. But I cannot ask you to stay here, in the cold ice, and look for him.

'Goodbye, Walton. Do not try to find the secret of life! I failed ... but perhaps another man will succeed.'

His eyes closed, and he pressed my hand. Then he became silent. Victor Frankenstein was dead.

It was late at night, and everything was quiet. I went outside and looked at the cold sea. My friend was dead, and I cried for him.

Suddenly, I heard a noise and I returned to Frankenstein. You will not believe what I saw! The monster was standing next to the bed, looking at Frankenstein's body. I have never seen anything so ugly and terrible. Long hair hung over his face. His skin was dry and yellow, like old paper.

'Oh, Frankenstein,' cried the monster, 'will you forgive me? But you cannot answer me – you are cold and dead.'

The monster looked at me. I closed my eyes, because I did not want to see his face. But I spoke to him.

'Why are you sorry now? Frankenstein is dead, but you came here to kill him!'

'Do not worry,' he said. 'My crimes are finished. I will not do any more evil things. Frankenstein suffered, but I have suffered too. Frankenstein created me, then he sent me into the world without love. Everybody hated me when they saw me. Nobody wanted to be my friend. So I learned to be evil. I killed everything that Frankenstein loved. That was my revenge.

'And now he is dead, and I must die too. There is nothing more for me to do. I will leave your ship immediately, I must go and die in the ice, as far away as possible.'

With these words, the monster said goodbye to me. Then he jumped off the ship into the cold water, and was lost in the darkness.

Readers usually agree that both Victor and his monster were bad. But which of them was worse? And did they also do good?

1 Work with another student. Choose one of these parts and make notes. Then have a discussion.

| Student A | Imagine that you are Victor. Prepare to defend yourself. Were you responsible for everything that happened? Did you also do good and bring happiness? |

| Student B | Imagine that you are the monster. Prepare to defend yourself. Were you responsible for everything that happened? Did you also do good and bring happiness? |

Notes

2 Choose two students from the class to stand up and make their defence in front of all the other students. Each should speak for three to five minutes. Other students can then ask questions and give their opinions.

3 Which speaker defended himself or herself best? Have a vote: Who was the more evil of the two, Victor or the monster?

4 Discuss, as a class, if other people were also responsible. For example,
   • did Victor's family and friends do enough for him?
   • do other scientists make terrible discoveries? Why (not)?
   • should university teachers know more about what their students are doing?

Work with another student. You are reporters for a Geneva newspaper and you are going to write about the life and death of Elizabeth Lavenza. This is the beginning of the report.

Murdered
on Her Wedding Day

The strange, sad story of the
girl who grew up with
the Frankenstein family.

1   Make notes about her life under these headings:

Notes

Her early life; how she came to live with the Frankensteins

The time that she spent with Victor and Henry

William's death and Justine's trial

Victor's illness and strange activities at university

Her continuing love for Victor and the family's plans for them

Victor's return, the wedding and her death

2   Now write your newspaper report on another piece of paper.

Mary Shelley wrote this story in the early 1800s. In those days the science of medicine was very simple. Of course it was not possible to make a monster from parts of dead bodies. It is still not possible now. But doctors and scientists today have made wonderful discoveries. They can often make people well again by giving them body parts from another person, alive or dead.

1 **Look at these parts of the human body. Which of them (✓) can be taken from one person and put into or onto another person?**

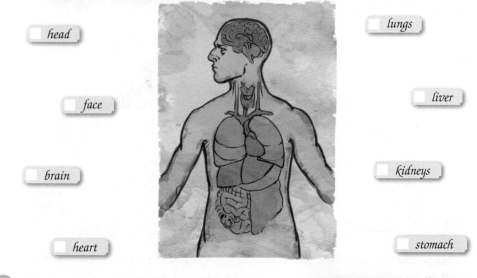

☐ head

☐ face

☐ brain

☐ heart

☐ lungs

☐ liver

☐ kidneys

☐ stomach

2 **This man is Dr Christiaan Barnard. Find out about him and answer these questions.**

a Which country did he come from?

....

b What did he do that made him famous?

....

....

....

c In what year did he do this? ....

d Who was Louis Washkansky?

....

3 Imagine that a pupil at your school is very ill. His heart is not working well.
The doctors say that he needs a new one. He has gone to a big hospital in the
city. His parents are not rich and cannot visit their son very often. As a class,
you decide to make some money for the boy's parents.

a Read these ideas and discuss them in groups. Which idea will work best? Which
one will make most money? Can you think of another, better idea?

* Have a sale of things that you don't need—
  books, clothes, toys, other things.

* Have a fun race through the town.
  People pay for each kilometre you run.

* Have a dance at the school.
  People pay for tickets.

* Students offer to do jobs for people
  in the town.

* Have a football match between the students and
  the teachers. People pay for tickets to watch it.

b Choose one idea and make plans. How will you do it? What will you need? Who
will do what? Make notes.

Notes

4 Discuss how you will tell people about your project. Then make a poster that you can put up in your school and in your town. Use the space below for your poster.

Remember to tell people:

- why you want this money
- what you are going to do
- when and where it will be
- what you want people to do

heartproject

5 Your project was a big success and you now have some money for the boy's parents. Write them a letter. Tell them that you are sorry about their son's illness. Tell them what you have done, and why. Tell them about the cheque that you are sending them.